WITHDRAWN

W9-BTR-020

minedition

Michael Neugebauer Publishing Ltd. Hong Kong

Text copyright © 2015 by The Jane Goodall Institute

Illustrations copyright © 2015 by Feeroozeh Golmohammadi

Rights arranged with "minedition" Rights and Licensing AG, Zurich, Switzerland.

All rights reserved. This book, or parts thereof, may not be reproduced in any form
without permission in writing from the publisher.

The scanning, uploading and distribution of this book via the Internet or via any
other means without the permission of the publisher is illegal and punishable by law.

Please purchase only authorized electronic editions, and do not participate in or
encourage electronic piracy of copyrighted materials.

Your support of the author's rights is appreciated.

Michael Neugebauer Publishing Ltd., Unit 23, 7F, Kowloon Bay Industrial Centre,

15 Wang Hoi Road, Kowloon Bay, Hong Kong. e-mail: info@minedition.com

This book was printed in July 2015 at L.Rex Printing Co Ltd 3/F., Blue Box Factory

Building, 25 Hing Wo Street, Tin Wan, Aberdeen, Hong Kong, China

Typesetting in Papyrus.

Library of Congress Cataloging-in-Publication Data available upon request.

ISBN 978-988-8240-49-4 (US)

ISBN 978-988-8240-36-4 (GB)

10 9 8 7 6 5 4 3 2 1

First impression

For more information please visit our website: www.minedition.com

Jane Goodall

We pray,
above all, for Peace
throughout the World

Art by Feeroozeh Golmohammadi

minedition

We pray
to the Great Spiritual Power
in which we live and move
and have our being.

We pray
that we may at all times keep
our minds open to new ideas
and shun dogma;

that we may become ever more
filled with generosity of spirit
and true compassion and love
for all life;

that we may strive to heal the hurts
that we have inflicted on nature

and control our greed for material things, knowing that our actions are harming our natural world and the future of our children;

that we may value each and every human being for who he is, for who she is, reaching to the spirit that is within, knowing the power of each individual to change the world.

We pray for
the children who are starving, who
are condemned to homelessness,
slave labor, and prostitution, and
especially for those forced to fight,
to kill and torture even members
of their own family.

We pray for
the victims of violence and war,
for those wounded in body
and for those
wounded in mind.

We pray for
the multitudes of refugees,
forced from their homes
to alien places through war
or through the utter destruction
of their environment.

We pray for
suffering animals everywhere,
for an end to the pain
caused by scientific experimentation,
intensive farming,
fur farming,
shooting,
trapping,
training for entertainment,
abusive pet owners,
and all other forms
of exploitation.

such as overloading
and overworking pack animals,
bull fighting,
badger baiting,
dog and cock fighting
and so many more.

We pray for
an end to cruelty,
whether to humans or other animals,

for an end to bullying
and torture in all its forms.

We pray
that we may learn the
peace that comes with
forgiving and the strength
we gain in loving;

that we may learn to take nothing
for granted in this life;

that we may learn to see and
understand with our hearts;

that we may learn to
rejoice in our being.
We pray for these things
with humility.

We pray
because of the hope that is within us,
and because of a faith in the
ultimate triumph of the human spirit.

We pray
because of our love for Creation,
and because of our trust
in the Great Spiritual Power.

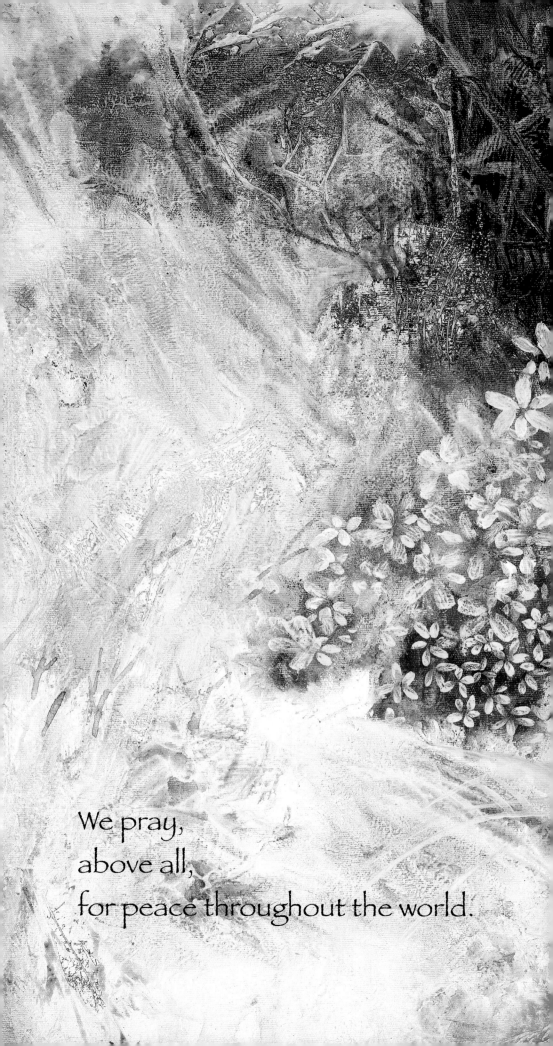

We pray,
above all,
for peace throughout the world.

Jane Goodall
UN Messenger of Peace

We all yearn for a world at peace. We are all horrified and saddened when we think of the violence in the world today—violence against one another and violence toward the natural world.

Our hearts go out to all the hundreds of thousands who have been killed, wounded or forced to flee from their homes. With the ever widening gap between the "haves" and the "have nots," there is a huge number of people whose basic needs are not being met, whose voices are not being heard. When they become desperate and sometimes violent, unscrupulous leaders can then exploit them for their own political gains.

Perhaps we cannot influence soldiers to lay down their weapons or governments to ground their missiles; but we can take the opportunity of the International Day of Peace to think about it, talk and make our views known.

And what about our right to live in peace with the natural world? We can think about how we live our own lives. Are we doing our best to live in harmony with nature? Do we care about the size of our ecological footprint? This matters, because lasting peace between peoples will never come about unless we learn to respect and live in harmony with nature.

Natural resources such as timber, wildlife and plants are not infinite, and our wasteful and thoughtless abuse of these is causing horrendous damage to the environment and blighting the future of life on earth. As Gandhi said, "Earth provides enough to satisfy every man's needs, but not every man's greed." If people are starving with no way out of poverty, they will hardly join our fight to protect the natural world for the benefit

of humans and other animals for generations to come. At the Jane Goodall Institute, we believe that every one of us can make a difference. Our programs help people to struggle out of poverty on the one hand, work to curb the excesses of the wealthy on the other, and try to find ways to slow down human population growth. Together, let us help humanity move to a future when "The Right of Peoples to Peace" becomes more than a slogan, but rather the foundation of a culture of peace for all.

Jane Goodall, Ph.D., DBE
Founder, the Jane Goodall Institute &
UN Messenger of Peace

THE JANE GOODALL INSTITUTE

"Only if we understand can we care
Only if we can will we help
Only if we help shall all be saved"

Jane Goodall PhD, DBE
Founder - the Jane Goodall Institute
& UN Messenger of Peace

The Jane Goodall Institute was first established in the USA in 1977, and there are now JGI offices in 27 countries.

Funds raised enable the Jane Goodall Institute (JGI) to support many programs including the ongoing research into chimpanzee behavior, now in its 55th year at Gombe National Park, Tanzania. We secured the support of communities located around Gombe and in other chimpanzee habitat further south through our TACARE program that improves the lives of villagers in a holistc way. And we have created sanctuaries for chimpanzees orphaned by the bushmeat and live animal trades. In addition to our projects in Tanzania, we have programs in Burundi, Democratic Republic of Congo, Kenya, Republic of Congo, Senegal, South Africa and Uganda.

JGI also works to improve the conditions of captive chimpanzees and other animals.

The Jane Goodall Institute needs your help.

For further information and to find the nearest office, visit
www.janegoodall.org

ROOTS & SHOOTS

When the seed of a big tree starts to grow tiny roots and a
tiny shoot appear. Pick it up – it seems so weak. Yet the roots, to
reach the water, can work through rocks and eventually push
them aside. And the shoot, to reach the sunlight, can work
through cracks in a brick wall and eventually knock it down.
Imagine the rocks and the walls as all the problems humans
have inflicted on our planet, both environmental and social.
Hundreds and thousands of roots and shoots, hundreds and
thousands of young people around the world, can break
through these walls. Together we can change the world.

"Every individual matters
Every individual has a role to play
Every individual makes a difference"

Roots & Shoots is Jane Goodall's global conservation and
humanitarian program for young people of all ages.
It began 25 years ago with just 12 high school students in Dar
es Salaam, Tanzania and there are now groups in more than
135 countries around the world. Members are empowered to
become involved in hands-on projects of their choosing in three
areas: one for the local community, one for animals (including
domestic animals) and one for the environment we all share.

Roots & Shoots works to break down the barriers that we create
between people from different religions, cultures, nations,
between rich and poor, old and young, and between us and the
natural world. As often as possible we bring older students
together from around the globe to discuss making this a better
and more peaceful world.

When Dr. Jane Goodall was made a UN Messenger of Peace by
UN Secretary Kofi Annan (and later reappointed by Secretary
General Ban ki Moon), it was decided that each September all
groups around the world would be encouraged to celebrate the
UN Day of Peace.

for further information about Jane Goodall's Roots & Shoots see
www.rootsandshoots.org

Feeroozeh Golmohammadi

is among the few Iranian illustrators who have revived
the ancient traditions of Iranian miniaturists. Her
systematic study of the works of these stunning artists
has provided an opportunity for her to present a
relatively little known aspect of Eastern art to the world.
Her illustrations—full of decorative elements combined
with human and animal forms—create an air of
mystery that recalls the characters of the legendary
One Thousand and One Nights.

As a graduate in Interior Design from the Tehran Poly-
technic, Golmohammadi has skillfully employed
various artistic techniques over a thirty-year career.
Her works have attracted widespread critical attention
at various biennials and children's book exhibitions
held throughout the world—particularly for her inno-
vative use of Eastern motifs. Through the course of her
artistic career, Golmohammadi has won scores of
prizes in numerous international exhibitions. Her international fame has increased with her being awarded
the prestigious Ezra Jack Keats International Award.

Golmohammadi showed talent from a young age, and she was always drawn to art classes, an interest that culminated in the study of interior design and numerous jobs creating artwork for children's magazines and television programs. When she tried her hand at picture book illustrations, her very first book won a prize, and she knew this was the career for her.

While she began with the techniques of Iranian miniaturists, Golmohammadi's distinctive techniques include a wide array of artistic styles, resulting in artwork that's drawn keen interest from beyond the borders of her native land.

As the French art critic Janine Despinette puts it, Feeroozeh's illustrations are created "...in an atmosphere surprisingly out of current events and at the same time quietly modern." Thus she is neither a traditional artist nor a modern illustrator.
Her work is one of a kind.

Golmohammadi lives in Tehran with her family, and she teaches art classes for children and adults alike. She says, "War, bloodshed, injustice and cruelty break my heart." She dreams of a world where peace abounds and where all our painful boundaries melt away, so that we see that we're all one people. She believes that if we all pray for this peace to come, one day that dream can be realized.